Last of the Cake

Alison Mace

Last of the Cake

© Alison Mace

First Edition ISBN: 978-1-913329-23-5

has asserted her authorship and given her permission to Dempsey & Windle for these poems to be published here.

All rights reserved. No part of this publication may be reproduced, stored in a retrieval system or transmitted in any form or by any means without the written consent of the author, nor otherwise circulated in any form of binding or cover other than that in which it is published and without a similar condition being imposed on a subsequent purchaser.

Published by Dempsey & Windle
15 Rosetrees
Guildford
Surrey
GU1 2HS
UK
01483 571164
dempseyandwindle.com

British Library Cataloguing-in-Publication Data

A catalogue record for this book is available from the British Library

For Michael

Acknowledgements and thanks

Thanks are due to the editors of the following publications, where the poems named first appeared:

About Larkin, journal of the Philip Larkin Society
        ('Baggy', 'In the Wild Wood', 'Love Talking')

Matter, student creative writing magazine of Sheffield Hallam University, 2005
        ('Overboard')

What the Peacock Replied, Dempsey &Windle, 2019,
        ('At the End')

Extraordinary Forms, 2007
        ('My tiger')

Transitions, Grey Hen Press, 2005
        ('Hearing a robin')

CONTENTS

I Centenarian

Philip at sundown	9
Lifeware	10
Too soon for bed	11
The spring fire	12
Uncle, goodbye	14
Hearing a robin	15
Outing to Keighley Tarn	16
Young Philip	17
At the end	19
To Philip, *in absentia*	20

II Other Poems

Glad to be female	25
In Reid's Café	26
Baggy	27
My tiger	28
Moment	29
Love talking	30
The score is in the score	31
In the Wild Wood	32
Last tea-time – Goole, Yorkshire, 1937	33
Diagnosed	34
Overboard	35
Till death part them	36
Last of the cake	37
Third eye	38

Centenarian

Philip at sundown

The sun rides down the winter afternoon
and casts on rug and hearth a glowing square
that flows up stonework, course by course, till soon
it floods with glory every surface there,
then bathes the mantelpiece, slides upward – fast
beyond it, fast – until the plunging sun
is swallowed by the land; and day is past,
bright hearthstones faded, sombre night begun.
The old man sits and watches, smiles, and calls
his son to marvel with him at the sight;
he loved the day, but even as it falls
accepts with equanimity the night:
he knows his own day's dark will not be long
in dawning; and his faith in light is strong.

Lifeware

Nine glasses – sherry, wine, water; side-plates, three;
dinner-plates, soup-bowls, Grandma's Spode tureen,
delicate cut-glass dishes; the cutlery –
heavy, ornate, antique – items, eighteen.
And now the saucepans, this greasy tin; a cup
or two, and the gravy-boat – how can there be
so very much to do, in the washing up
of a Sunday lunch for Philip and you and me?
Well, we needed to do it right. It's the only meal
he enjoys, and he loves to see his fine oak table
rich with the family stuff – it helps him feel
his life is still as it was. And if we're able
only to give him that, it makes his day.
So, shift yourself! – all this is to put away.

Too soon for bed

November indoor dark
gropes in coat-cupboard,
fumbles a blank hearth,
clamours for lamps, red coals,
toasties, cosy curtains
and soon an early night.

But just step out to where
damp twilight cools your cheek,
grass still gives back green,
moon climbs a steep path
and pigeons wheel yet, pale
over a peopled park.

The spring fire

Such a bright late-March Sunday,
hot, but for breeze, as summer
– a day to clear the terrace
of two dark winters' leavings:
scur of plant-straw; branches
frost-nipped, cast in storms;
cobwebs, bark-dust, earth-dust.

So, behind the bowed,
incontinent, pane-releasing
wreck of a greenhouse, build
a cleansing fire for spring.
Bank as we go: dry slivers
flaring, armloads of sticks
brittle as cinder-toffee,
snapping with puffs of dust.
Now we scrabble the web
of skeleton stems off earth,
heave grey ash-boughs on.

Round and round I walk,
up-ending logs the fire's
burnt short, to the crackling crown -
not breathing, a scarf of smoke,
in league with the fleering breeze,
chasing me as I work,
laughing to see me kippered.

The pile slumps, fading; only,
as light drains out of the sky,
the last dry twigs, poked in
to tap its sunk heart, kindle
the life the fire-heap harbours.

Morning reveals it cool
except at the core, soft alp
of raw, sweet ash, which now
we'll mix and stir with humus
to spread on the starving ground
and feed a further spring.

Uncle, goodbye

Edwardian, comical, he looks like something
out of an early *Punch*: shaky old man,
spread stance to steady him, his slept-on hair
too long – but there's no scissor sharp enough,
in this old house, to shear him – wearing a vest,
loose, long – his shimmy, Grandma would have called it –
and nothing else except a crooked smile.
'Alison wants,' I hear my cousin tell him
carefully, slowly, trying to penetrate
without indignity his plastic ears,
'to say goodbye. She's leaving.'   'Well – she can!'
He edges forward, hand on the bedroom rail,
to kiss me: these days our cheeks, our eyes, are level,
his noble height deformed and shrunk to mine.
I glimpse him, back in fifty-something, mowing
his parents' lawn, as now we do for him –
sports jacket, neat moustache, the handsome head
of dark-brown backswept hair: he valued that,
he paid me then (an avaricious child)
ha'penny a hair to pull the grey ones out.
For years I kept him dark, and no-one knew –
a game we shared with glee. No less today,
my nearly-naked nonagenarian,
the uncle he always was to me, I love him.

Hearing a robin

May. And it's hailing here. I text my friend:
Just off 2 hospital w Aged P
4 modern hearing-aids.
                      Well, she texts back,
I'm sitting in my garden in the sun
watching a robin. Hearing it too, no doubt.
Will digital technology, I wonder,
let Philip hear a robin?
                    Hope so, she taps.
And so do I. (If so, we'll have to watch
ourselves, not talk about him while he's there.)
Philip and robins . . . every year he'd tame one
to eat out of his hand.
 Waiting outside
now. And he's hobbling out, and beaming too!
Hope it's still sunny where u r – cos here
the sky has cleared, the sun is beating down.
Robins are opening their beaks to sing.

Outing to Keighley Tarn

He stays in the car, well-blanketed, expressing
himself abrim with pleasure:
'Oh, what a lovely sight!' waving a hand
at the cold tarn, bent trees, dark overcast.

I slam the door on the warm, take a few steps
as usual, over draggled grass
from parking-strip to water, then start lobbing
fragments of fossil toast over his sightline
to tempt the wheeling, squabbling gang of gulls
to entertain him.
They almost never catch one. The odd coot
lunges and gulps. Ducks come paddling in.
Fixed smile behind the glass. I brush off crumbs
as picnic-leavings stir to a blade of wind.

I slam again, on the cold; slide in the key.
'Oh!' he begins, 'I do appreciate this!'
The engine's warming up. We're off again:
'I feel such gratitude . . . at ninety-eight . . .'
I know what's next. 'Philip, you're more than welcome –'
'– at ninety-eight, to have such loving care . . .'
I back away. '– an outing every day,
or almost every day . . . that splendid room . . .'
First gear; all clear behind? Let's go, then. '– means
so much to me. And I've been giving thanks . . .'
Third gear to fourth: nearly up to the limit.
'– been praying all the morning . . .' Here we go! –
my foot's down hard, too hard. '– just giving thanks . . .'
Here it comes, then, the crest: '– so fortunate not
to have to spend my last days in a Home!'

Another premium paid. We coast downhill.

Young Philip

Young Philip was fourteen and lanky, a twin,
not much of a scholar compared with his brother,
a loner, a thinker, a cross-country runner;
spent days on a golf-course in spring '21,
Perivale golf-course, following, searching
for lost balls to sell where he could.

But he's pushing his luck, because one day a hand
comes grappling into the back of his collar.
Hard hand turns him, flaring eye fixes him,
threats of the Pro – the Pro who will beat him,
criminal boy, for trespass and theft.
He's frog-marched along, by way of a bridge,
a plank on a ditch – where he seizes his chance,
he wrenches away from the furious golfer,
who loses his footing and dignity, rolls
in the trickling ditch, while Philip takes flight –
a twenty-yard lead by the time the man rises
and follows – as fast as the practised young runner –
as fast, but not faster. They sprint up the fairway,
on past the clubhouse and into the lanes
where there's nowhere to hide, or dodge, or take cover.
Now Philip, well into his wind, has his measure:
he'll never catch up, but he won't give up either.
The Pro and his vengeance give Philip the spur,
his lithe adolescent legs warm to the chase.

He starts to enjoy it, he leads the fraught golfer
for miles – and the golfer keeps going – he's fit,
quite fit for his age, and he'll chase the young varmint
as long as his lungs and his muscles hold out.
Three miles, perhaps more, and now they're in Harrow,

where young Johnny Betjeman walks to his parties
in sandals from Heal's, in decorous clothing
not heard of in Philip's large household in Ealing.
Now Harrow is known to the hunted, known better
than ever it was to the flagging pursuer.
He's into an alley, he's crouching and grinning
to hear the fooled hunter wheeze off out of hearing.
But Philip daren't go by the way that they came.
He walks home the long way, returning at twilight.
His mother's been anxious, he's scolded; he's smiling.

For months he avoids all connection with golf,
but he's run for his manhood, and holds it for life.

At the end

At last it ended: you,
panting, unheeding, not
knowing your son, or me,
had stamped the final seal
on your neat century.

The frightened, grateful shell
that you had grown to be
once no one leant on you
and need was all you knew –
that travesty of you fell,

and, fallen, cleared the view,
letting us see you stand
witty and strong and kind,
and suddenly we know
our deeper loss is – you.

To Philip, *in absentia*

We won't come with you to the crematorium.
Forgive us, dear Philip, please,
we think you would understand –
we want to look after your guests, your many friends
at the neat church where your funeral is just over;
they're old – not a hundred years old like you,
but old enough, and now sufficiently moved
to be glad of our helping hands,
arms to hold on to up the church hall steps,
chairs pulled out for them at the trestle tables,
trays brought over to them with funeral food.
And they want to talk, they want to know us, your nearest:
'I never had a daughter', one frail woman says,
'but if I had I'd have liked her to be like you.'
So we're happy we thought of it, to bring you back
here, to set off from your own church, even though
it wasn't your church for long, just from the time
your other church nearby went happy-clappy,
with banjos, you insisted, banjos and hugging,
not to your sober taste.

So no, we did not see you
slide off between dark velvet curtains;
were spared the turning-aside of eyes, the trying
not to envisage what must happen next.
But now, at your banjo church, your family meets
for a final ritual, the burying
of a small, stylish urn: your last remains.

But it's all over so quickly,
the vicar's formal words, and the little urn
popped into a small hole dug before we came;
a trowelful of pale Hertfordshire soil
thrown in, tamped down; and the two men who did it
and even the busy vicar, seem to expect
that we'll go now, duty done. But we stand on,
even have to explain
that this is the end indeed, that we need to stay
to watch the cut turf lifted, fitted back
into its small square bed; and tidied, smoothed –
that we have to see you safely covered up.

Other Poems

Glad to be female

I'm happy to be a woman,
glad I was born female
in an age when women can work,
are respected for their talents,
accorded praise where it's due –
mostly – not always; we'll get there.

And I'm glad of our special privileges,
to grow my hair long if I want to,
or shear it – and never to lose it;
to look as I choose, wear trousers
or skirts, or brash make-up, on a whim.
It's not like that for men.

I'm at ease in soft skin, glad
to be a natural talker, sharer,
equal giver and taker among friends;
and grateful to have been a little girl
playing kitchens and cribs, and blessed
with a blind calm confidence in her future.

But any little boy - how I feel for him,
so tender, just another young child –
betrayed by bold testosterone:
height, muscle, cracking voice, rough chin
call him too soon a man, child he still is
banished, weeping in private, locked in.

So I rejoice still in my womanhood:
to have received nature's best honour,
the chance to carry new life –
with no responsibility for design,
charged only with staying well, and safe –
gently to the gate of an awesome world.

In Reid's Café

Strange what a difference height makes,
height and a sheet of clear plate glass.
Blowing on coffee to cool it, I see through the steam
lives below in the street leap into sudden focus.

An old man turning the corner – not really old,
now I glimpse his face. But weight, and unlucky gait
have wrestled him right down. I feel his certainty
like a cold draught: that this is his last spring.

Three girls, afloat on a cloud of hormones:
so indisputable which is the leader –
admired and copied, loved and hated for her looks.
Both the others will have better marriages.

A family now. Boychild lolls in the buggy.
Big girl skips ahead, she loves her bouncy hair.
It's thin little sister, handle-clinging, I feel for –
not first, not boy, not baby, dull hair, glasses,
snapped at for tripping on slung shopping-bags.
I understand: this one will never be free.

Who sat above, I wonder, clairvoyant in coffee-steam,
watching me – six, blue hair-slide, leather sandals –
too anxious to cross the road? Was it clear then,
the whole unplanned, unique, surprising route
that's brought me to this quiet café window?

Baggy

'Bags I!' we'd cry, claiming our certain right
to the biggest biscuit, first read of a book,
upstairs on the bus the coveted front seat.
Easy entitlement! You got in quick –
'Baggy!' – that's all it took. If another kid
beat you to it, well, that was all right too,
it was settled, agreed by all, you knew where you stood –
no silly messing about – 'You first' – 'No, you.'
Later, it wasn't so easy – exams, a job,
the boy you fancied – 'Baggy' didn't get those.
You learnt to negotiate, compete with the mob
for even a little of what, if you could, you'd choose.
In age, can you bag good health? Not to be lonely?
No pain? A peaceful death among friends? If only.

My tiger

My tiger, in her portrait, pauses mid-pace on grass,
behind her the tropical dark; her heavy, handsome head
turned to appraise the lens, exhibits, model-style,
her whiskered chops just parted, pink tongue peeping,
and the alien, gold eyes in a full-on stare.

Beautiful, my Kamrita. I have a stake in her:
monthly I stow away in a banker's draft,
fleet above wide oceans, mountain ranges, deserts,
come to my great cat sleeping, caress her massy paw,
stroke sparks from the smooth nap of her splendid side.

Fooled? Is this only a donor-charming scam?
The cash buys fence-posts, stun-guns, desert-rovers,
wages for sweating lads in tattered shorts –
oh, is Kamrita real, or a catch-all name,
handy seductive image, striped fund-raiser?

What if? For me still, slack in her rich, loose skin,
she sleeps, shields me in the crook of a warm foreleg.
Her clean-cat smell, her purring sigh, her warmth transport me
also to sleep, in a dappling forest of bright birdsong,
of whispering monkeys, under a million leaves.

Moment

Listen. This is a moment when
some newborn gasps cold air, expels it screaming,

when snow roars down a blinding Alpine slope
to sweep away new corpses,

when in some steaming forest or broad, blank waste
a creature reaches the still point beyond purpose –

lion morphs into meat in a cloud of insects,
tortoise inside its hard shell withers to dust;

a moment when millions eat, starve finally, or
are sleeping, weeping, mating, killing, laughing:

a sphere of action so immense
I cannot hold it to me; shrink apart

to this my personal moment: the blank glare
of a building buffered by snow,

when all that is possible is
to hear the crackling silence, breathe, accept
my quiet, only pulse.

Love talking

He speaks, and she hears in his voice
the warmth of his back in bed,
friendly roughness as foot meets foot,
the dark warm tide engulfing.

She's tuned to the sudden jolt
as his elbow seeks its place
or shaking of ribs as he reads
to send himself down smiling.

Waking to window-grey,
her fretful night-work fading,
she hears in his gentle breathing
permanence, safety, love.

The score is in the score
West Side Story at the Proms

How it starts – with a scrap of tune
vital, provocative – 'You lookin' at me?'
'I bite my thumb, sir.' Right from those nimble notes
a knot is lying there, slack cords on the asphalt –
going to be tugged tight, going to unravel
sure as Shakespeare – tragedy, pure, unstoppable.
Jets and Sharks brimming with hot blood,
spurting life, fire in their muscles, opposed –
a rumble brewing for certain. The score's in the score.
Maria and Tony ignited, she feels pretty,
for sure she does, but her very music betrays her –
gun-shots suggest themselves as she starts to sing.
There's a place for them . . . sure, a place that was always
their separate graves. We know from the first note
of this yearning duet, the score. And when it comes
weaving back at the end, floats like gun-smoke
above the broken bodies on the street,
it's what we have always understood at our core.
Verona. Manhattan. Oh, America.
Gee, Officer Krupke,
there's nothing you could have done.
Blood, fire, star-soaring hope,
seeds of catastrophe and rage and grief,
and pity, the aching pity of it:
they were all in place from the start.

In the Wild Wood

Tonight they are walking in the Wild Wood
with Ratty and Mole. Snow is falling. The Rat,
they know, is afraid, however boldly he strides
forward, trying not to look at the eyes.

Eyes in hard faces staring from dark trees
are frightening, and they're afraid as well –
the little one anyway. But she's all right,
curled into Daddy's arm. She can see the book.

The others sprawl on her bed. The Wild Wood
has to be done some time, you can't escape it.
It's tough. You can't know what the whistling means,
whose are the eyes, whether you'll make it home.

Daddy reads on. They've found the Badger's door . . .
and now they're having supper, everyone's safe,
Badger is big, but kind, a bit like Grandpa –
and the little one's asleep on Daddy's lap.

He lifts her up. lays her head on the pillow,
pulls the warm quilt close, right to her chin.
The two go blinking off to their own beds.
All's well. The Wild Wood is floating away.

The household sleeps. Outside, a wind gets up
and whistles softly through the trees. Leaves fly.
The garden sycamore, grown huge and strange,
extends a twig to tap against the wall.

Last tea-time - Goole, Yorkshire, 1937

We're sat at the table – Nan and old Auntie, Gramp, and us kids.
   And it's quiet. Nobody talking.
Gramp, he's started already, greedy, not being polite,
   and Nana's looking daggers,
she's got that face on again, mouth in a thin straight line.
   She's not been so well this year.
But she's made us a grand tea – sausage and beans and fried bread.
   She's not got started on hers.

Mam should have come, could have shown her face, Nan said to Gramp.
   But she never comes on a Monday –
she works, she's a nurse, she lives with a poorly lady in town,
   a Catholic lady, Nan says.
Well they think I don't know, but I've listened when Mam's been talking to Nan:
   a lovely place, she says.
But a Catholic place, says Nan. You know we've allus been Chapel.
   Nuns! – what do they know?

It's different tonight. Sort of still. In the front room there's two big bags.
   Our clothes! I had a look.
So I've got a sort of idea that I know what's going off.
   Our Pete doesn't know. Too young –
four, and he can't even cut up his sausage right, he's a baby.
   He'll go in the babies' part.
But I'm seven soon, so they're putting *me* in the big lads' house.
   I s'pose we'll be all right.

I'll still go to school, I think, but not the same one as now.
   I hope they'll let us paint –
I'm doing this picture, a big one, to make me remember tonight –
us, all sat round the table,
Grandpa and Auntie and me and our Pete, and Nan looking sad,
   and sausage and beans for tea.
They think I don't know, but I've heard what they've said and I do.
   I don't think I want this bun.

Diagnosed

Understanding you're to be fast-tracked,
hearing the grave-eyed consultant say
there is certainly an abnormality,
you shift, instantly and without panic,
to a far extreme: leg, breast, eye –
whatever it was you could learn to live without it.
Thousands do. Think of Helen Keller.

Now brain gapes wide, ingesting apocalypse:
trivial, your small plight, beside
trickle of glaciers, gases killing the sky,
febrile fingers poised over switches;
and at your eye-corner dark images
of brash new giants smirking
politely as their installations
leap up to crowd horizons.
Terminal, you cry, wallowing; it's all
coming to an end, and soon.

Breathing, back in daylight, you find
the cautiously-proffered hope of a cure
pure bathos. And now the world
as it still is hardens out of the blur,
and here are the things about it
that have to be dealt with:
hot fear; the knife, oblivion;
loss irremediable, dependence, pain.
This staring ring of anxious, loving faces.

Overboard

Flailing, already you can picture
the tall stern check, the ungainly turn, you
tossed in the wash a choppy minute or two,
then grappled aboard, dried off –
the embarrassment – but safe
for a joky hour back at the captain's table.

It's a puzzle: the stern still dwindles,
reaching to a hard gunmetal-grey line
that goes right round
and nobody's looking back.
Dimness and chill grow louder
steadily as the ship fades on your eye.

Bad joke. Moon stares, impartial as charity.
Best dip your face and die. Sorry,
that's not in the rules, insist the decencies,
even though they have dumped you.
No. You must tread this irksome ocean
till the hard line draws tight and takes you.

Till death part them
Cambridge Botanic Garden

He brings her here because she used to love
the place so much, when she was well. A chore,
getting her started, now that she can't move
unaided: washing, treating each of those sore
places she wakes with, easing off the socks;
the loo, her clothes, her make-up – for he feels
she'd value her old standards. Bed stripped, crocks
cleared and the laundry on, at last he wheels
her carefully down the ramp, to Bateman Street,
and in under the cedars with their cones
like eggs. How she loved those, used to greet
them laughing with delight. Today, her bones
sag, eyes droop and close. With sober tread
he turns for home. They both long for bed.

Last of the cake

Their faces brightened
because I'd brought a cake.
We've all enjoyed it. 'More?'
I ask, looking at them in turn.

They smile again. The elder,
deaf, and with deficits
of other kinds, that come
with being ninety-six,
accepts a quavering sliver
with 'half a cup – enough.'

His brother too; no halves
for him, though. 'That last bit –
think it wants eating up –
let's have it.' And he does.

There isn't much.

Even a crumb is good.

Third eye

A bright sheer plaque of light
leaps up from the shower-washed flagstone yard
making me shrink back – blinding my eyes
to everything that waits beyond, behind:
for that a third eye's needed.

Just on the other side
a tight-packed wedge of smooth lawn lies,
cut in like peat to the neat flower-bed, where
a lithe striped cat springs at a cloud of gnats
brilliant in shafts of sun.

Further, against the hill,
the eye picks out that high blue house,
paled almost to white by a thousand dawns,
where I pause snatching breath whenever I toil uphill
to glimpse the far winding Severn.

Now eye veers to the right,
flies high over the flashing counties, northward –
my Pennine fields, bleached pastel-green by winter;
then higher still, to the hard line of the moor,
limestone, and dazzling sky.

Are you, then, heart, there still?
No – pledged to friends, here in the border country
where shining Wye and Severn meet the sea.
Eye, stay for me there by Wharfe and Aire;
watch, and I will return.